Who would have thought poems about dead husbands, distanced fathers, and social awkwardness could evoke such a sense of hope, and even laughter? This is the genius (no, "genius," while accurate, feels too stuffy…) this is the magic of Laura Foley's latest collection of poetic narratives. Manifesting the profound through everyday details (dog licks…sandy sheets….hospital kisses!), *Joy Street* isn't just a heart-filling read, but a place you'll want to return to time and time again.
—Joni B. Cole, author of *Toxic Feedback, Helping Writers Survive and Thrive*

These poems are like crystal: delicate, sharp, clear, full of light. They radiate joy. They are a praise song to "Clara," to love, to finding love again after loss. More that that, they mark the speaker's continuing search to find her own identity (and by inference, our own search for ours). That they do so with such carefully chosen images and words, with such honesty and lyricism, is proof of Laura Foley's depth of spirit and talent. Read these more than once as I have; each reading gives new discoveries and pleasures.
—Patricia Fargnoli, author of *Winter*

These poems revel in, and model, peace, contentment, gratitude, joy, and joyful humor. Few convey so much, so vividly, with such brevity, as Laura Foley. Read "Drift," for masterful imagery, metaphor and wit in two sentences, and the love poems for sentimentality-free sincerity. The few personal details show us this poet earned her wisdom and mature romantic relationship, growing beyond anxiety to an increasingly serene existence; achieving eros and agape by learning self-love, that most difficult, most rewarding, of loves.
—April Ossmann, author of *Anxious Music*

Joy Street

Joy Street

Laura Foley

Headmistress Press
2014

ISBN-13: 978-0692237557
ISBN-10: 0692237550

Cover Art © 2012 Barbara Perrine Chu
Primavera
Original 12" x 16" mixed media
Prints available from Pink Pagoda Studio / Society 6

Cover & book design by Mary Meriam.

Published by Headmistress Press
60 Shipview Lane
Sequim, WA 98382
Telephone: 917-428-8312
Email: headmistresspress@gmail.com
Website: headmistresspress.blogspot.com

To Clara

Contents

Wild Women Do

I don't recognize her at first,

this stranger-become-friend

on the long-distance coach: our wayward exes

and teenage children, her work

with PTSD vets, my chaplaincy in New York—

she asks if I'm divorced,

and when I gleefully say, *Yes,*

then, *I mean No,*

then, *He's dead—*

we slide off our seats

in the back of the bus,

writhing with wild hilarity,

by the coffee tray and apples.

Queer

I sit all morning, then through lunch, as the café empties and fills.
Young woman by the window stays too, cool girl I've a secret crush
on, so studious with her law books. *Environmental,* I hear her say, to
someone else. I want to weave my hands through her hair, but I don't
know her name. Once, I said *Hi,* as she passed, and she smiled back,
seizing me with dumb fright, as usual, when it's someone I like.
Because we're both women, I've learned this means I'm queer. I like
how the word defines me, explaining a lifetime of feeling different,
not wanting to flirt with guys, or wear high heels. Now, she's sitting
with her headphones on. Just a moment ago, she yawned.

Ghost Street

People speak of wanting to relive a day in their youth, wishing the dead alive. I look up the narrow airshaft to the windows of my childhood home, see myself in a short school frock, one ordinary evening, silver candlesticks flickering the mahogany table's length, white-uniformed maids bending over platters in the cavernous room, my stomach twisting as Dad demands I pronounce *shoe*, stares at me with eyebrows raised, determined to cure my lisp, mother and sisters listening, forks suspended. I look up the narrow airshaft of my childhood home, with no desire I dare pronounce.

Near Miss

I wake up with a knife

between my ribs

near my heart.

Upright, I'm fine,

feed the dogs,

let them out, and in.

Back in bed,

the jab returns at 5 a.m.

I think of Sue's cancer,

my dad's heart disease,

my mom, post-stroke.

I think of Dickinson's blank of pain,

Homer's poisoned arrows,

the sea of anguish flooding me,

a wave I ride till it passes—

fate driving by me

in its red jalopy, en route

to someone else.

Dinner Party

I don't know anyone here except my new partner Clara. I haven't spoken a word in two hours, but now her lawyer colleagues discuss the hostess' mother's ashes stashed upstairs in a closet and I think— *Great!* I will leap in with the story of how we buried my husband in the front yard, dug the hole ourselves—*Yes,* it's legal in New Hampshire, *Yes,* I got a vault. I'll sound smart, resourceful, witty, and everyone will like me. I've been pretending I'm my quiet musician son, thinking deep thoughts, but feeling bored and awkward, a pained smile cracking my face. Now I've missed my chance, the husband says vaults are a terrible idea, because you want the body to decompose into earth and tree roots, and I think: *OMG, I've buried him badly.*

But I'd confuse them if I did contribute, since no one knows I was married, never mind widowed, husband buried in the yard. Someone's talking cat coffins, asking, *maple or pine?*—or shiny walnut and Thai mahogany with hot pink satin lining—someone else has a pet cemetery with wind chimes to remind them of Fluffy. Clara, shy and quiet too, smiles as I do all through dinner, though she tells me later she could have explained about ashes, the ease of letting go.

Gender

In my dream, the seductress,
naked from the waist down,
displays her penis, soft
and gray, curved as a shell.
When she enters me,
I aspire to my own androgyny,
like these three women
sitting in the café near me, at ease
in suspenders, crew cuts, tattoos,
which can't disguise
the cat-like softness of their eyes.

Hologram

My left hand, deep in fur,

rubs her dog, ears, chest and neck;

the other hand holds a book.

Though she's away at work,

my mind won't focus

while its memory reads

our bed's crumpled sheets,

but my hand goes deep.

New Dog

I have a new dog, same temperament, same color and wise eyes, but an urgency all her own. We search weeping vines and budding shrubs for access to the glimmering river, but we're stopped by a steep ravine, treacherous mud obscured by jungle ferns, knee-high grasses—I try another way, making a new path through old hills. She pulls me forward, hard as I can manage with the leash, and I like it.

Aubade

Though pine trees toss all night in their feathery beds as I do,
they seem at peace, where I've yet to learn to sleep with you,

wondering whether your warmth keeps me awake,
or the stirrings of eternity.

Even trees sleep in midnight air, whose stillness seems endless,
when you wander dream streets without me.

Your wandering next to me, without me,
teaches why the faithful fear limbo.

At dawn, a bright spring junco
nips suet from the feeder

as you greet my waking, spring's scent rising
from our snow-cold stream.

Springtime in the Grocery Store

We're shopping, gathering ripe pineapples, kiwis, oranges, when she leans in to me, coos: *I love it when you talk fruit,* and I whisper, *Mango, mango, mango,* so she swoons, and soon we're rolling on the tiled floor together, between the dairy aisle and spicy condiments.

The Poet Volunteers

Any carpentry experience? Don't worry, we'll teach you everything. They fit me
with a heavy leather belt, measuring tape, fat wrench sagging my waist.
Stooping, I follow five men into the dark, cramped, understory of a
listing house, moldy walls, too-close ceiling. As they explain the job,
my eyes seek the far-off exit hole, tiny eye of sunlight not meeting
mine. Trying not to imagine beams caving in, I fasten on his words,
Did you say 'sistering the boards?,' but feel faint, hearing the tragic calls my
children will receive, kitchen collapsed on my head. *You'll be fine,* the
foreman promises, leading me out, pairing me with a handsome young
mason, who encourages, *There must be a poem in this,* teaching me to slap
wet goo on bricks, leave my fingerprints on seams of stone.

No GPS Necessary

I love you, I say, as we leave

the hotel room,

as we take the elevator down,

and stroll city blocks

to the hospital,

as we walk the antiseptic corridors,

and she's wheeled away,

as I return to Joy Street,

where yesterday

she said those words to me.

Freudian Quips

On our first Psych. 101 conference call of the semester, we hear from
James, standing in a corn field in Ohio or Iowa, where phone
reception's not so hot, but doable if he doesn't use video. Meghan
from Texas appears onscreen looking slightly depressed, or maybe it's
the darkness, her room in shadows behind her. White-haired
Professor Janus looks intent, a little tired, tinkers with the video. I
scan her crammed bookshelves till Marlene joins us, but her camera's
gone wonky, a small gray rectangle, with her name on it—when Peggy
logs on, geometrically red as a Rothko, the audio starts echoing and
Professor Janus jokes the shivering gray panel looks like a map of *the
unconscious, the unconscious, the unconscious,* and I chime in—*or outer space,
outer space, outer space,* making the sleeping dogs lying beneath my desk
in Vermont stir restively, as James from Iowa or Ohio says it's
beginning to rain, ending our first conference call.

Like Teenagers

Clara's home resting, a little unwell today. Tomorrow we'll see her doctor, follow-up after brain surgery. But even when her sodium levels were dangerously low, when we knew she could go at any moment, we had a good time: put calming music on, held hands. She recounted morphine dreams, colorful bears and totem poles, stories I wrote in my notebook. We giggled at staff behind their backs, the beady eyes of the fellow resembling an ostrich wearing a neck brace, the resident attempting broken Spanish for us, and the flustered night aide blurting: *I'm supposed to check your breathing,* when she caught us kissing.

Rare

I've loved my freckles

since I was three,

when a stranger bent over me,

praising my *sun-kissed* cheeks.

Today, a doctor freezes

my *skin damage*, blistering

a piece of me away,

changing how I frame it.

A friend praises my distorted feet

as *medieval*, pointing to prophets

on stone facades. When the barber

calls my hair *fine*, I hear

excellent, as in *fine wine*.

Once, I wanted fish *well done*,

but *rare* calls me now.

Gelato

She buys me gelato,

my favorite,

but eats it

on the way home.

It was so cold, so delicious,

coffee sweet cream,

I'm so sorry,

she says with a kiss,

and hands me

the empty dish.

Hindsight

I happen after the photo
of my emaciated father
standing on a ship's deck,
dark hair combed neatly to the right.
He's just endured four years of war,
POW for the Japanese, starved,
water-boarded.
One feature commands our attention;
my partner names it, *his survivor eyes,*
just like mine.

Angle of Repose

We moved the bed

so the head faces north,

a wisdom we read,

from India.

We dislodged a ghost,

her husband,

who on these sheets

three years ago expired.

We altered the angle

of our repose

and sleep all night

at peace, entwined.

We wake to morning hills,

trees, a green expanse,

a gentle, dappled light

new to us.

Voyeur

She's so happy planting beans,

the latest strand of peppers,

garlic, eggplant, seed potatoes

in our Eden.

I love to watch her,

on her knees in ecstasy.

Lullaby

Heart-startled awake to rain

hammering its monstrous fists,

demanding entry, I think, *Apocalypse!*

Clara half-wakes, reassuring me.

But my children far away?

Okay too, she soothes to sleep,

her wedding hand on mine.

Maternal Semiotics

It was only eight weeks, but I missed the world since becoming a
mother, so I bundled the baby up, took him to hear a lecture in the
grand hall at my alma mater. I wore a fashionable grey wool cape
which worked for my furtive purpose. The Famous Writer lectured
on: semiotics, physics, Italian roses—background noise muffled by
sounds of sucking, unparsed poetry rising from my breasts.

Not Humming

On the forced march from Tientsin to Woosung, our Marines, ordered silent—*No humming or singing,* snapped the Japanese, as the men trudged a hundred miles to prison. My father not humming the whole of four winters, or to my knowledge, since.

On Sense

After two beach weeks, sun-tanned and sandy, I perch, air-deprived as
a pet canary, amidst piled books, diligently marking paper with pen,
while anybody with any sense enjoys the air at the nearest body of
water, as I follow the urge to make sense of surf, to make waves that
may outlast memory.

Dream Interpretation

I'm attacked by a hyena who's attacked by a swan who flies away with the offending beast, as an angel might, white-plumed and feathery-strong. My analyst advises it's a paradox, the angel, a savior, the bestiality of hyenas, the renewal of death. *Let its teeth penetrate, feel your liver tearing, like Prometheus. The hyena rips out the dead you, the girl who learned to be still. Let her die, be reborn, speak her truth. And yes, be the swan too!*

The Land of Happy

Sometimes all this grinning feels so strange, I just lie on the porch doing nothing energetic, just lolling on the sun-warmed wood, letting the dogs lick my face, while the din of loneliness fills other ears.

Drift

I eye-roll Aunt Lizzie, who can't see me over the phone, tell her I'm

dating a woman now, but at ninety she's adrift in uncharted seas, till I

say we may marry—and she crests the wave, her kind old voice

soothing: *Oh, but Laura, you're still attractive to men,* grasping the rudder

with practiced hands.

Midpoint

This night, in an eternity of such nights,
we escape the illusion of an unmoving home
to watch stars getting born and dying
in violence and fire,
forging new galaxies for who knows whom,
or what, or why.
We settle under our car's open roof-become-lens,
this shivery midnight on a windblown hilltop,
the horizon below us.
Have some chocolate, she offers,
tucking a blanket around us,
midpoint of stillness
between our own fiery poles.

Concord

Over an omelet and toast Clara's made for us,

I ask if she minds my morning silence,

a time when spirit composes,

and if I listen quietly enough, I hope my pen

will translate its music for my mind.

Clara says we're listening to a symphony of us,

with a bridge between our solos.

After Winter

We stroll lawns

just now free

of four month's snow.

We press

so close,

we throw

one shadow.

A Good Life

I didn't realize I was

a *stay-at-home* mom,

but knew I didn't know

how to get a job,

English Lit. degree,

my kids full of need

and fun, the best

I could have done,

I know,

now they're grown.

Bay Winds

Sandy from a day at the beach,
we sleep on top of our sheets,
windows open wide,
little feet running over us.

Grace

The famous white-haired poet orders for a group, frappuccinos, mochas with skim milk, double soy lattes. The young barista gets confused, scribbles hurried notes. The poet rests a worn, compassionate hand on her youthful shoulder, letting her know she has all the time she needs to breathe. I await my turn, thinking I'd like to be like her. Not the famous part. The graceful part.

Late-Night Low Tide

Around our feet,

the scritch-scritch-scratch

of claws on sand,

ancient sounds

of midnight rounds,

of seemingly solid ground

shifting under us:

revealing worlds

below our own.

Acknowledgments

My thanks to the editors of the following publications, in which these poems first appeared, sometimes in slightly different versions:

Black Fox Review: "Freudian Quips"
Nicelle Davis' *Umbrella Project:* "Lullaby"
Poems for a Queer Revolution: "Queer"
Poetry Nook: "Dream Interpretation"

Notes and Thanks

"Grace" is written in memory of supportive and warm neighbor-poet, Grace Paley.

Thank you to all the great baristas and owners of Tuckerbox Café, for creating a vibrant work space, and the best cappuccino anywhere; to Joni Cole for writing classes, ongoing mentorship, community and laughter; to April Ossmann for amazing editorial acumen; to Susan McKenzie for ongoing guidance and splendid dreamwork; to my children, Aaron, Billy and Nina, for growing up so beautifully; to Carol, Clyde, Cristen, Pam, Anne, Sue and Heather, for lively poetry gatherings; to Barbara Perrine Chu for joyous artwork; to Mary Meriam and Risa Denenberg for believing in *Joy Street* and giving her a home.

Thank you, Clara, for that first wink, and then how you entered my life.

Thank you furry friends, Arlo, Alys, and Chloe, for your attentiveness, and our long romps in the woods. (P.S. Chloe: please don't eat this book.)

About the Author

Laura Foley is the author of four previous poetry collections. *The Glass Tree* won the *ForeWord* Book of the Year Award in Poetry (Silver), and was a finalist for the New Hampshire Writer's Project's Outstanding Book of Poetry. Her manuscript, *Night Ringing*, was a finalist for the Autumn House Poetry Prize. Her poems have appeared in journals and magazines including *Valparaiso Poetry Review, Inquiring Mind, Pulse Magazine, Poetry Nook,* and *Lavender Review.*

She won Harpur Palate's Milton Kessler Memorial Poetry Award and the Grand Prize for the *Atlanta Review*'s International Poetry Contest. A volunteer chaplain, yoga teacher, and creative arts facilitator in hospitals, she lives on a woody hill in Vermont with her partner, Clara Giménez, and their three dogs. Please visit her website for book information or more poems: laurafoley.net or follow her on Twitter: Laura Foley@laurafoleypoet.

Also by Laura Foley

The Glass Tree (Harbor Mountain Press)

Mapping the Fourth Dimension (Harbor Mountain Press)

Syringa (Star Meadow Press)

Made in the USA
Lexington, KY
20 July 2014